First, You Explore

Young Palmetto Books

Kim Shealy Jeffcoat, Series Editor

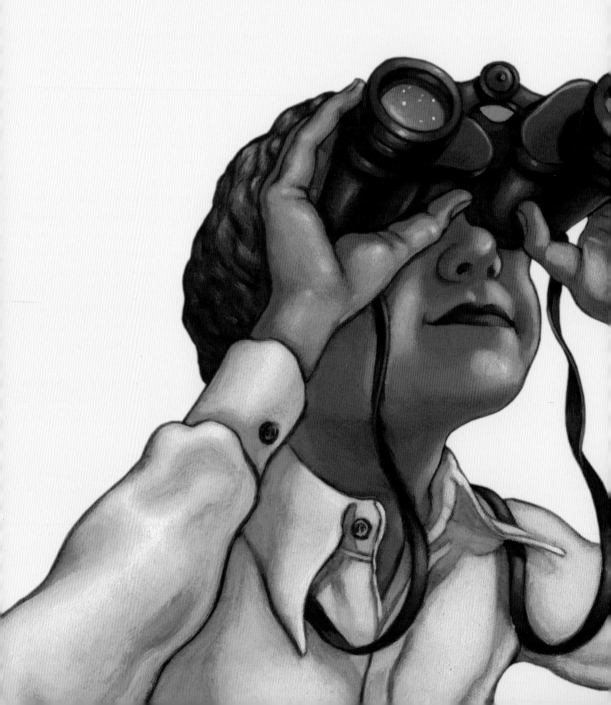

FIRST, YOU EXPLORE

The Story of the Young Charles Townes

Rachel Haynie

Illustrated by Trahern Cook

The University of South Carolina Press

Dedicated to Penelope and Kate as well as Mazie and Walt and other inquisitive children everywhere, especially those in the family of Dr. Charles Townes

Do exploration. Do things that are new and different. Sure, some of them are going to fail, but new and different things are likely to pay off most. Don't be too worried about failure. Be willing to take some chances.

Charles Townes

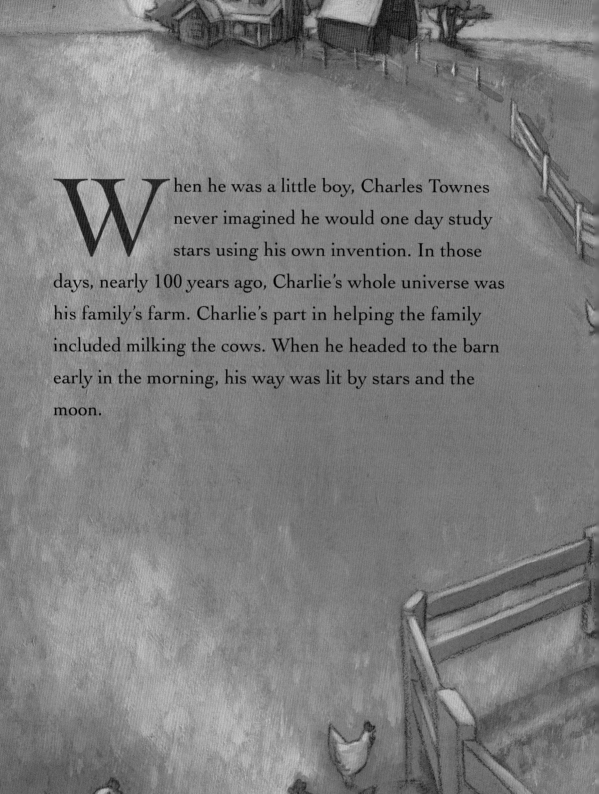

When he was a little boy, Charles Townes never imagined he would one day study stars using his own invention. In those days, nearly 100 years ago, Charlie's whole universe was his family's farm. Charlie's part in helping the family included milking the cows. When he headed to the barn early in the morning, his way was lit by stars and the moon.

Milk in the Townes
children's glasses came
from the cows. From the
barnyard came the meat
served at their dining table. In their
orchards the Townes grew fruit. In their
fields they grew crops, some to sell, some to eat.

What Charlie learned on the family farm turned out
to be his first lessons for a life in science.

Splashing in the creek running through the farmland, Charlie and his older brother, Henry, found tadpoles, fish, salamanders, and turtles. Sometimes the boys brought home their discoveries for the aquarium their father made and set up in the yard.

The brothers also explored the woods that surrounded the farm.

Did birds roosting in thickets or perching in tall trees no longer need their nests? Charlie sometimes climbed out on sturdy limbs to check. If the nests were empty, he gathered them for his front-porch collection.

There birds' nests took their places alongside unusual rocks, chunks of moss, bits of pottery and stone tools—including arrowheads—made by Native Americans long ago, and pieces of rusted metal unearthed by the sharp blades of the plows used to ready the ground for planting farm crops. In Charlie's time plows were usually pulled by work animals, not the tractors and other motorized farm equipment we have today.

Studying creatures in their natural habitats was a pastime Charlie and Henry never tired of. But often, just as their study was getting interesting, their subjects flitted, slithered, or scampered away.

To continue their study of the ones that didn't escape, Charlie and Henry often took living creatures home and kept them in cages they made from sticks and vines.

Their mother neither fussed nor fumed when her sons brought their natural-science collections into the house. She even let them keep caterpillars in their rooms so they could watch them form chrysalides, the protective coverings in which caterpillars change into their adult shapes. Then the boys waited for butterflies to emerge and fly. Butterflies and moths belong to an order or group called *Lepidoptera*, which in Greek means "scaly wings." Nature arranges these scales in colorful designs, unique to each species, giving the butterfly its beauty.

Henry especially liked bugs–or insects. He kept his head down, looking for crawling things, and when he grew up he became an entomologist, a scientist who studies insects.

Charlie looked out for anything new. Across open fields he gazed at the distant Appalachian Mountains' foothills. And he looked up to the skies. In summer Charlie went back outside after supper, and at dusk he watched fireflies flit about, winking on and off. Once dark- ness fell, he recognized his favorite con- stellations far away. If only he could get a closer look!

One clear night, his father gave Charlie binoculars and showed him how they worked. Mr. Townes believed astronomy, the study of the universe beyond the earth, had much to teach his second son. By turning the focus wheels of the binoculars with his thumbs, Charlie brought objects in the sky closer. The heavens seemed almost within his reach.

With his new tool for exploring, Charlie sometimes crawled up on a rock near the creek running through the family's farmland. It was a quiet place to think and observe nature. Lizards sunned nearby. With the sun beaming down, he searched the horizon for new wonders. To learn something new, he'd ask himself: "What do I see today that is familiar? What am I seeing that is different?"

Although his binoculars were a valuable asset to his exploring, his intelligence was his most important discovery tool. Being good with his hands helped him in his explorations, too.

Picking cotton from its bolls, tinkering around with spare parts to build a wagon, and milking the cows all helped him become good with his hands. Charlie didn't know it yet, but such knowledge would come in handy through his lifetime in science.

His family encouraged his tinkering. When Charlie was ten years old, he wrote his older sister before she began her Christmas shopping and appealed to her to "buy out the hardware store." He already knew that science and building complemented each other. He needed more tools.

One day a clock maker whose shop was near Mr. Townes's law office had an old clock he couldn't fix. He thought the boys would enjoy working with it, so he gave it to Mr. Townes. Charlie and Henry took the timepiece apart and experimented with the clockworks, tarnished fittings and little brass gears. The old clock never kept time again, but tinkering with it taught the boys much.

In time Henry went back to his bugs, leaving Charlie to tinker with the clock.

Exploring together as well as apart created a healthy competition between the brothers. Henry wanted to make sure Charlie didn't copy any of his experiments. But Charlie had plenty of ideas of his own.

To keep straight which brother had an idea first their father used his legal skills. He advised his budding scientists to bring their newfound discoveries to him in writing. Then, for the small fee of one nickel each, he would gladly patent their ideas. The brother holding the patent had his ideas legally protected. Case closed!

The brothers continued to explore new things, outdoors and in. Sometimes they had only to plop down on their living-room floor. Within reach were magazines, guide books, maps, and encyclopedias that brought the world into their home. Playing school, with their older sisters—Mary and Ellen—as teachers, introduced Charlie and Henry to more new ideas. Each evening the family read together.

Among their favorite things to read were letters from Aunt Clara, who lived and worked in Japan—quite rare for an American woman in those days. Charlie and Henry soaked the international stamps off the envelopes and dried them before studying them carefully. Another collection began.

Their father sometimes brought home unusual coins from the bank near his office. With a magnifying glass, Charlie studied the letters and symbols on the copper or silver coins. Special coins went into yet another collection.

Sometimes Charlie went with his father to help out at the law office. Downtown Greenville, South Carolina, was

Downtown Greenville in the early 1900s. Courtesy of Greenville County Historical Society, Greenville, South Carolina.

emerging as a textile center and had many unusual things to see. The more Charlie learned, the more curious he became.

Walking to school each day, Charlie wondered what kind of rock he was kicking and whether the chunks of coal on the ground had tumbled off a train car. In school he asked more questions than most other students. Sometimes at recess older boys picked on him for being so interested in learning, but Charlie shrugged it off. Even in his vast universe, there was no place to worry about what a few kids thought of him.

In fact, his universe had begun to expand beyond the lessons taught by his elementary-school teachers, so his parents let Charlie skip seventh grade. In eighth grade he found that high school classes offered more challenges.

But throughout his school years, the traditional class-room was only one of his learning places. Explorations and studies he undertook on his own were just as enlightening.

Beyond the property surrounding his home, a favorite learning environment was the South Carolina coast.
When visiting relatives in Charleston, Charlie compared
and contrasted items he'd collected in the Palmetto State's
upcountry, where he lived, with those found along the
shore. He looked forward to visiting the Charleston
Museum, America's first museum.

(left) The museum Charlie visited in Charleston. Courtesy of the Charleston Museum, Charleston, South Carolina. (below) A skeleton of an Atlantic right whale on display at the Charleston Museum. Courtesy of the Charleston Museum, Charleston, South Carolina.

Visits to his other grandmother gave Charlie opportunities to explore the North Carolina mountains. Stones he picked up, looking first to see what lived beneath them, felt different in his hand than those he collected back home. He also noticed that the shapes of leaves floating fast in the cold mountain water were unlike those that drifted slowly past the family farm.

While splashing in a stream, he spotted a boulder much like his thinking rock back home. Sitting on this new rock, he pondered the theory of relativity by Albert Einstein, who had received a Nobel Prize for his important work in theoretical physics in 1921. Even at such a young age, Charlie understood Einstein's mathematical equation. As he sat on that rock, he even thought he'd found a flaw in science's most famous formula.

When he got hungry, Charlie stepped back from the equation long enough to eat lunch with his grandmother. Then he brushed off a few sandwich crumbs and headed back to his thinking rock—and Einstein's theory. Before the sun started sinking behind the nearby mountain, Charlie figured it out: Einstein had been right after all.

Another day at his grandmother's mountain cottage, Charlie returned to the nearby creek and caught an unusual-looking fish. Its colors and shape did not match any fish he had studied in books on the family bookshelf. He decided to pickle the fish in formaldehyde and mail it off to the Smithsonian Institution in Washington, D.C. He attached a note asking: "Can you tell me what kind of fish this is?"

Weeks passed. Finally Charlie got a letter from the Smithsonian. It read: "We think you have found a new species of fish. Can you send more?" But by then summer vacation had ended, and Charlie was back home in Greenville. His chance to net more fish for the nation's premier natural-history institution had slipped away.

He'd never know what kind of fish he'd caught, but he had learned that, if science became his life's work, disappointments and failures would be part of all exploration and discovery.

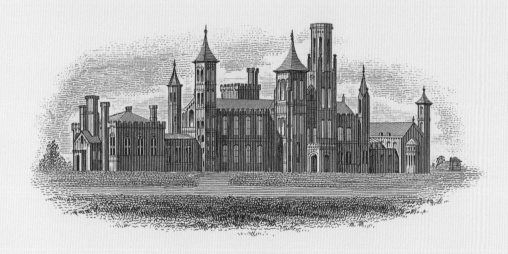

The bell tower at Furman University. Courtesy of Greenville County Historical Society, Greenville, South Carolina

When he was only sixteen years old, Charlie began college at Furman University, which happened to be just across town from his family's farm.

By his second year he was tutoring other students, working in the small Furman Museum, and selling apples from
the farm to earn money for college. That same year he
discovered physics was the field of science for him. He
explained his career decision to his parents by saying,
"It's logical and deals with the real world."

From the time Charlie first explored basic physics in a
Furman University lab, he has always had a lab in which
to explore, a place to test his theories. And outdoor thinking continues to be a favorite way to clear his mind too.

After completing the highest level of college studies,
Charlie started his career in physics at a New York City
lab. The science of microwaves, on which Charlie was
working, was important to communications, especially
during World War II. He learned that shortening wavelengths produced more powerful results than with longer
wavelengths. He explored ways to reach shorter and
shorter wave lengths.

Later, when he was a professor at Columbia University, he had been wrestling for a while with a research problem and had not yet solved it.

Then, as so many times before, Charlie was thinking outdoors, sitting quietly on a Franklin Park bench in Washington, D.C., early one April morning. Then it hit him! He figured it out!

The theory he worked out, once it was fully developed, led to the creation of the *maser*. The term *MASER* stands for Microwave Amplification by Stimulated Emission of Radiation. From the maser he later developed the laser.

A laser is a very intense, pure, and directional beam of light whose waves are coordinated in space and time. The name *LASER* stands for Light Amplification by the Stimulated Emission of Radiation.

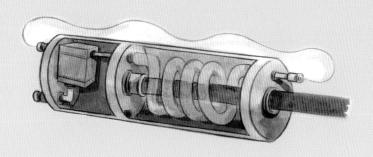

For his work on that idea, and how it would help the world, Charlie won the Nobel Prize in Physics in 1964. When he received that prestigious honor in Stockholm, Sweden, he still had no idea how many ways the laser would help humanity. Possibilities grew into realities as other inventors around the world developed uses for Charlie's best-known invention.

The principle of using a light source to produce heat is similar to using the rays of sun that pass through a magnifying glass. Lasers enable doctors to repair delicate tissue in the eye, and they help ships and planes to keep to the intended path. Manufacturers use lasers to cut through steel and fabric, and people can now communicate in ways not possible before the laser came into being.

In the second phase of his career—astrophysics—Charlie even used his invention to study the heavens. The precision that characterizes lasers makes it possible to pinpoint where stars are located. That way their composition can be determined.

Charlie is still exploring!

The Nobel Prize was established in 1895 by Alfred Nobel, whose many inventions include dynamite. Since 1901 prizes for physics, chemistry, physiology or medicine, literature, and the advancement of peace have been awarded to men and women whose work will help the world. A prize in economics was established in 1968 and awarded for the first time the following year. Recipients, who from then on are called laureates, receive a gold medal, a diploma, and a sum of money, which varies based on the Nobel Foundation's income during the year.

Timeline

1915 — Charles Hard Townes is born on July 28 in Greenville, South Carolina.

1931 — At age sixteen Charles begins college at Furman University, where his older brother, Henry, is already a student. The boys' father and uncle were also educated at Furman.

1935 — Furman University awards Charles Townes two degrees: a bachelor of science in physics and a bachelor of arts in modern languages: French, Spanish, German, Italian, and Russian.

1936 — Townes completes Duke University's academic requirements for a master's degree in physics; the degree is conferred in 1937.

1939 — Townes receives his Ph.D. from the California Institute of Technology and then joins the Bell Laboratories research staff in New York City.

1948 — Townes becomes an associate professor at Columbia University and continues his research in microwave physics.

1950 — Townes is promoted to professor at Columbia.

1951 — Townes comes up with the formula for the maser.

1952–1955 — Townes serves as chairman of the Physics Department at Columbia.

1955–1956 — Townes is a Guggenheim Fellow and a Fulbright lecturer, first at the University of Paris and then at the University of Tokyo.

1958 — Townes and Dr. A. L. Schawlow, who is married to Townes's sister Aurelia, show theoretically how masers can be made to operate in optical and infrared regions, establishing basis for the invention of what they call lasers.

1959–1961—On leave of absence from Columbia University, Townes serves as vice president and director of research at the Institute for Defense Analyses in Washington, D.C.

1961—Townes becomes provost and professor of physics at the Massachusetts Institute of Technology (MIT).

1963—Townes is Scott lecturer at the University of Toronto.

1964—Townes wins the Nobel Prize in Physics, sharing it with Nikolay Basov and Aleksandr Prokhorov of the Soviet Union.

1966—Townes resigns as provost in order to devote more time to research at MIT.

1966–1970—Townes heads the NASA Science Advisory Committee for the Apollo lunar-landing program.

1967—Townes becomes a professor at the University of California, Berkeley, where he continues astrophysics research.

1986—Townes retires as distinguished professor emeritus, but continues his research at Berkeley.

A Biography of Charles Hard Townes (1915–) for Parents and Educators

A physicist and Nobel laureate, Townes was born in Greenville, South Carolina, on July 28, 1915, the fourth child and second son of the six children born to Henry Keith Townes, an attorney, and Ellen Hard Townes. Charles grew up on a farm and was interested in natural history from an early age. He visited the collections of the Charleston Museum and was fascinated by the differences between plants and animals he saw on the shore and in tidal inlets and those of his own Piedmont region. He attended Greenville public schools and Furman University, where he received a bachelor of science in physics and a bachelor of arts in modern languages, graduating summa cum laude in 1935. Townes completed work for a master of arts in physics at Duke University in 1936 and entered graduate school at the California Institute of Technology, where he received his doctorate in 1939. He married Frances H. Brown of New Hampshire on May 4, 1941. The couple has four daughters.

As a member of the technical staff of Bell Telephone Laboratories from 1939 to 1947, Townes designed radar bombing systems during World War II. He subsequently joined the faculty of Columbia University, where he served successively as associate professor, professor, and chairman of the physics department from 1948 to 1961. On leave from Columbia from 1959 to 1961, Townes served as vice president and director of research of the Institute for Defense Analyses in Washington, D.C. He then moved on to the Massachusetts Institute of Technology (MIT), where he served as provost and institute professor from 1961 to 1966. In 1967 Townes became a professor at the University of California, Berkeley. He became university professor emeritus in 1986, but continued his research and teaching after retirement.

Townes's principal scientific work has been in microwave spectroscopy, nuclear and molecular structure, quantum electronics, radio astronomy, and infrared astronomy. He holds the original patent for the maser and shares to patent for the laser with his brother-in-law Arthur L. Schawlow. Townes conceived the idea of the "maser" (an acronym for "microwave amplification by stimulated emission of radiation") in 1951 and achieved the first amplification and generation of electromagnetic waves by stimulated emission in 1954. Four years later Townes and Schawlow suggested that masers could be made to function in the optical and infrared region. They dubbed these optical and infrared masers "lasers" ("light amplification by stimulated emission of radiation"). His pioneering work with masers and lasers earned Townes the Nobel Prize in physics in 1964.

During much of his career Townes has been a government adviser. In 1960 he was a founding member of the Jasons, a group of scientists who provide advice to the government regarding national issues involving science and technology. Townes served on the President's Science Advisory Committee from 1966 to 1970 and was chairman of the technical advisory committee for NASA's Apollo program until shortly after the lunar landing. He chaired committees on strategic weapons and the MX missile and has been an active member in the National Academy of Science. He has been active in helping to formulate advice given by the Papal Academy to the pope on issues of peace and the control of nuclear weapons.

Townes is the author of three books: *Microwave Spectroscopy* (with Arthur Schawlow, 1955), *Making Waves* (1995), and *How the Laser Happened: Adventures of a Scientist* (1999), as well as many articles. His achievements have been recognized with many awards and honors, including the National Medal of Science (1982) and no fewer than twenty-seven honorary degrees.

Mary S. Miller

Sources

Townes, Charles Hard. How the Laser Happened: Adventures of a
   Scientist. New York: Oxford University Press, 1999.
———. "A Life in Physics: Bell Telephone Laboratories and World
   War II, Columbia University and the Laser, M.I.T. and Govern-
   ment Service, California and Research in Astrophysics." Interview
   by Suzanne B. Riess. 1991–1992. Regional Oral History Office,
   Bancroft Library, University of California, Berkeley.

© 2010 Rachel Haynie
Revised edition © 2014 University of South Carolina

Hardcover edition published by Ellerbe Press, 2010
Hardcover, paperback, and ebook editions published in Columbia,
South Carolina, by the University of South Carolina Press, 2014

www.sc.edu/uscpress

23 22 21 20 19 18 17 16 15 14   10 9 8 7 6 5 4 3 2 1

Library of Congress Cataloging-in-Publication Data

Haynie, Rachel, author.
   First, you explore : the story of the young Charles Townes /
Rachel Haynie ; illustrated by Trahern Cook.—Revised edition.
pages cm.—(Young Palmetto books)
   ISBN 978-1-61117-343-7 (hardbound : alk. paper)—
   ISBN 978-1-61117-344-4 (pbk. : alk. paper)—
   ISBN 978-1-61117-345-1 (ebook)
   1. Townes, Charles H.—
Childhood and youth—Juvenile literature. 2. Physicists—
Biography—Juvenile literature. 3. Scientists—Biography—
Juvenile literature. I. Cook, Trahern, illustrator. II. Title.
QC16.T725H39 2014
530.092—dc23
   [B]   2013027982